MW01681579

Listen, my children, and you shall hear

The Midnight Ride of Paul Revere

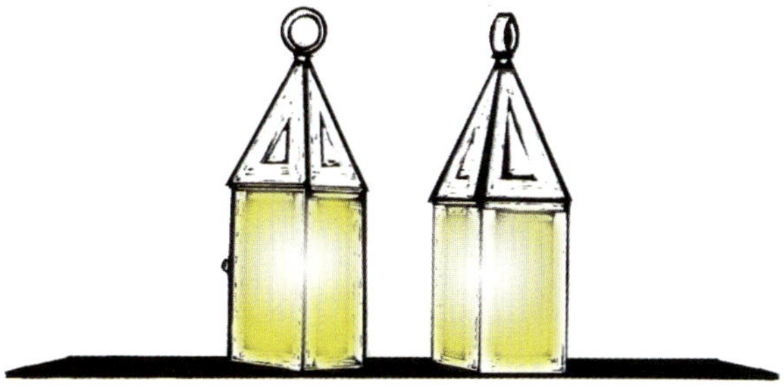

by Henry Wadsworth Longfellow
illustrated by Jeffrey Thompson

SCHOLASTIC INC.
New York Toronto London Auckland Sydney
Mexico City New Delhi Hong Kong

Listen, my children, and you shall hear
Of the midnight ride of Paul Revere,
On the eighteenth of April, in Seventy-five;
Hardly a man is now alive
Who remembers that famous day and year.

He said to his friend, "If the British march
By land or sea from the town to-night,
Hang a lantern aloft in the belfry arch
Of the North Church tower as a signal light,–
One, if by land, and two, if by sea;
And I on the opposite shore will be,
Ready to ride and spread the alarm
Through every Middlesex village and farm,
For the country folk to be up and to arm."

Then he said, "Good night!" and with muffled oar
Silently rowed to the Charlestown shore,
Just as the moon rose over the bay,
Where swinging wide at her moorings lay
The Somerset, British man-of-war;
A phantom ship, with each mast and spar
Across the moon like a prison bar,
And a huge black hulk, that was magnified
By its own reflection in the tide.

Meanwhile, his friend, through alley and street,
Wanders and watches with eager ears,
Till in the silence around him he hears
The muster of men at the barrack door,
The sound of arms, and the tramp of feet,
And the measured tread of the grenadiers,
Marching down to their boats on the shore.

Then he climbed the tower of the Old North Church,
By the wooden stairs, with stealthy tread,
To the belfry-chamber overhead,
And startled the pigeons from their perch
On the sombre rafters, that round him made
Masses and moving shapes of shade,–
By the trembling ladder, steep and tall,
To the highest window in the wall,
Where he paused to listen and look down
A moment on the roofs of the town,
And the moonlight flowing over all.

Beneath, in the churchyard, lay the dead,
In their night-encampment on the hill,
Wrapped in silence so deep and still
That he could hear, like a sentinel's tread,
The watchful night-wind, as it went
Creeping along from tent to tent,
And seeming to whisper, "All is well!"
A moment only he feels the spell
Of the place and the hour, and the secret dread
Of the lonely belfry and the dead;

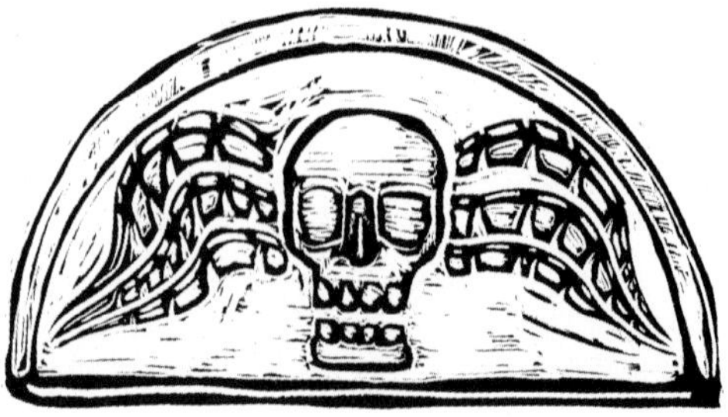

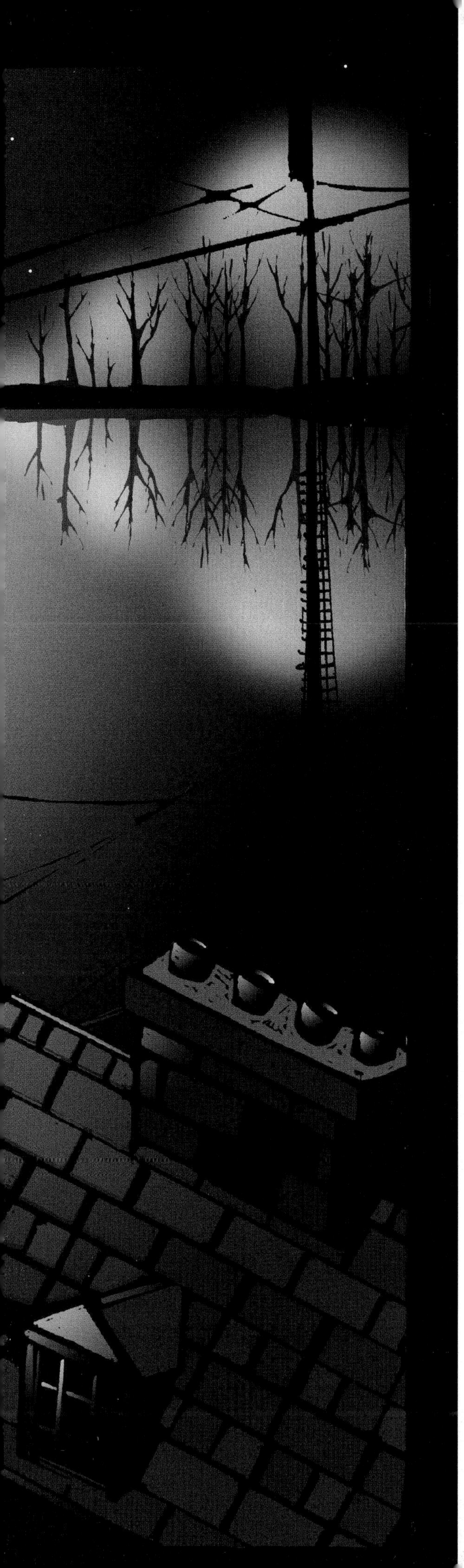

For suddenly all his thoughts are bent
On a shadowy something far away,
Where the river widens to meet the bay,–
A line of black that bends and floats
On the rising tide, like a bridge of boats.

Meanwhile, impatient to mount and ride,
Booted and spurred, with a heavy stride
On the opposite shore walked Paul Revere.
Now he patted his horse's side,
Now gazed at the landscape far and near,
Then, impetuous, stamped the earth,
And turned and tightened his saddle girth;
But mostly he watched with eager search
The belfry-tower of the Old North Church,
As it rose above the graves on the hill,
Lonely and spectral and sombre and still.
And lo! as he looks, on the belfry's height
A glimmer, and then a gleam of light!
He springs to the saddle, the bridle he turns,
But lingers and gazes, till full on his sight
A second lamp in the belfry burns!

A hurry of hoofs in a village street,
A shape in the moonlight, a bulk in the dark,
And beneath, from the pebbles, in passing, a spark
Struck out by a steed flying fearless and fleet:
That was all! And yet, through the gloom and the light,
The fate of a nation was riding that night;
And the spark struck out by that steed, in his flight,
Kindled the land into flame with its heat.

He has left the village and mounted the steep,
And beneath him, tranquil and broad and deep,
Is the Mystic, meeting the ocean tides;
And under the alders, that skirt its edge,
Now soft on the sand, now loud on the ledge,
Is heard the tramp of his steed as he rides.

It was twelve by the village clock,
When he crossed the bridge into Medford town.
He heard the crowing of the cock,
And the barking of the farmer's dog,
And felt the damp of the river fog,
That rises after the sun goes down.

It was one by the village clock,
When he galloped into Lexington.
He saw the gilded weathercock
Swim in the moonlight as he passed,
And the meeting-house windows, blank and bare,
Gaze at him with a spectral glare,
As if they already stood aghast
At the bloody work they would look upon.

It was two by the village clock,
When he came to the bridge in Concord town.
He heard the bleating of the flock,
And the twitter of birds among the trees,
And felt the breath of the morning breeze
Blowing over the meadows brown.
And one was safe and asleep in his bed
Who at the bridge would be first to fall,
Who that day would be lying dead,
Pierced by a British musket-ball.

You know the rest. In the books you have read,
How the British Regulars fired and fled,—
How the farmers gave them ball for ball,
From behind each fence and farm-yard wall,
Chasing the red-coats down the lane,
Then crossing the fields to emerge again
Under the trees at the turn of the road,
And only pausing to fire and load.

So through the night rode Paul Revere;
And so through the night went his cry of alarm
To every Middlesex village and farm,–
A cry of defiance and not of fear,
A voice in the darkness, a knock at the door,
And a word that shall echo forevermore!
For, borne on the night-wind of the Past,
Through all our history, to the last,
In the hour of darkness and peril and need,
The people will waken and listen to hear
The hurrying hoof-beats of that steed,
And the midnight message of Paul Revere.

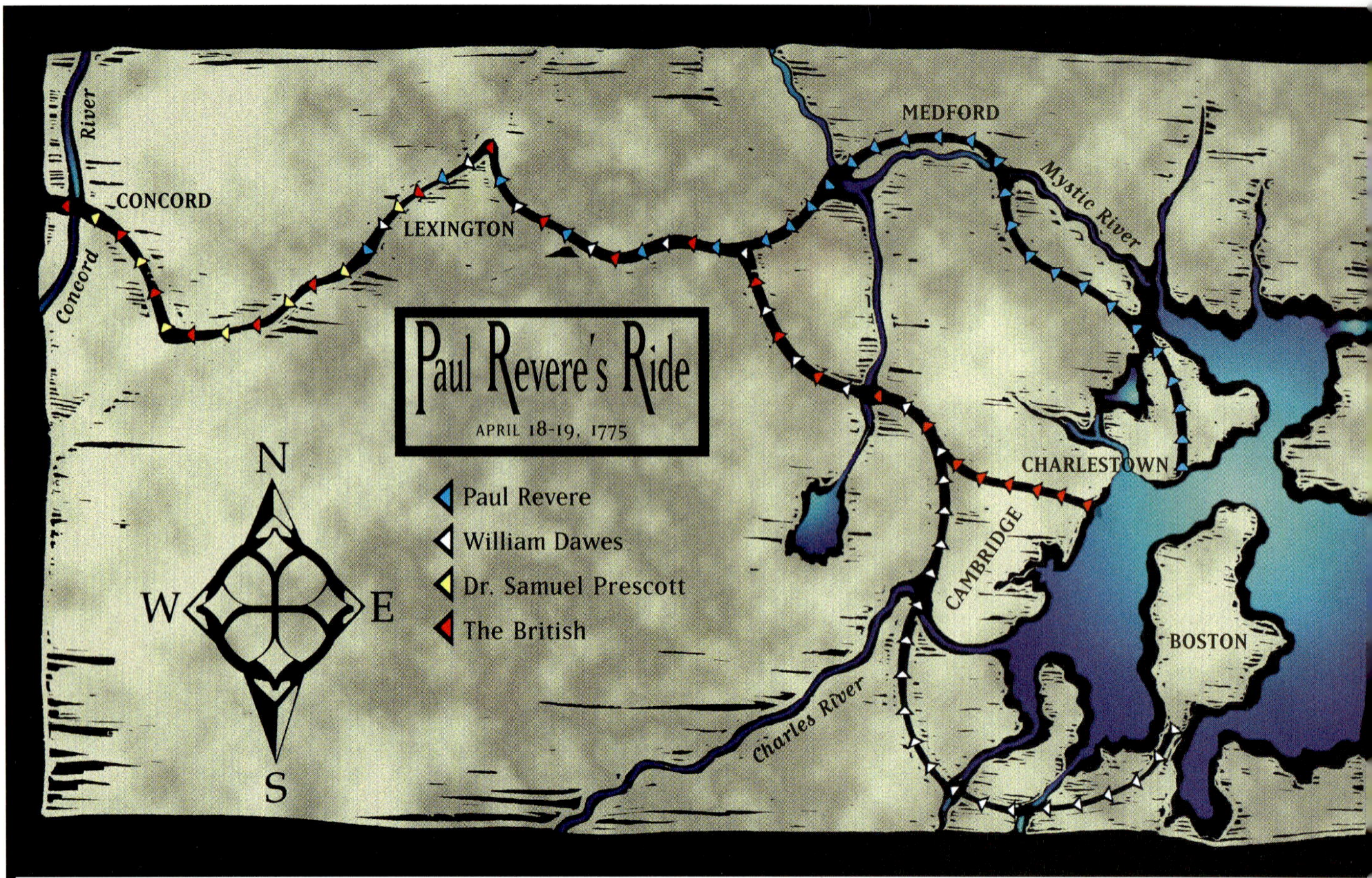

Historical Note

Henry Wadsworth Longfellow's stirring poem of the events leading up to the battle of Lexington and Concord made Paul Revere a folk hero for generations of Americans. But Longfellow's poem is not an actual historical account. In fact, Paul Revere never even made it to Concord. What was the true story of Paul Revere's ride? It goes like this:

The American Revolution had not yet started on the 18th of April in 1775. So far, the colonists had only been protesting and arguing to try to get England to treat them more fairly. But there were many who thought that the colonies should break away from England, and some had started to collect guns and ammunition so that they would be ready to fight if necessary. The British knew the rebels were preparing for war and were worried. Whenever they could, they seized guns and ammunition from the rebels to keep them from growing too strong.

On the night of April 18, a British force of about 700 men left Boston. They were planning to surprise the town of Concord and seize colonial ammunition stored there. But patriots had been spying on the British troops for some time and had caught wind of the plan. That night silversmith Paul Revere and shoemaker William Dawes set off to sound the alarm. Besides alerting the countryside, they also hoped to warn two rebel leaders in Lexington: Samuel Adams and John Hancock.

Revere had been an active revolutionary for some time. He had helped plan the Boston Tea Party, and some think that he participated in it as well; he had spied on British troop movements around Boston; and he had ridden back and forth to Philadelphia several times, carrying news to and from the Continental Congress.

The weekend before, Doctor Joseph Warren, one of the last leaders of the independence movement still in Boston, had assigned Revere and Dawes to spread the news of the British troop movements. Worried that he might not get out of Boston safely, Revere asked a friend to hang signal lanterns in the tower of Christ Church in Boston. The signals would let patriots across the river know whether the British were marching out of Boston by land or rowing across the Charles River "by sea." That way, even if Revere was stopped from leaving Boston, others could carry the news to Lexington and Concord.

But in the end the signals weren't necessary. Revere avoided capture, and was rowed across the river by two friends. In Charlestown he borrowed a horse and set off for Lexington, stopping at each house to call the patriots to arms.

Arriving at Lexington at about midnight, Revere alerted Adams and Hancock and then was joined by Dawes, who had taken another route from Boston. They started for Concord. Just outside Lexington, another patriot, Dr. Samuel Prescott, joined them. The three men continued toward Concord, stopping at every house to spread the alarm.

On the way, a British patrol stopped the men and tried to arrest them. Prescott knew the area well and escaped immediately by jumping his horse over a stone wall. He galloped on to Concord. A little later, Dawes fled back to Lexington on foot. Revere was not so lucky. The British held him for a couple of hours and then let him go without his horse. He never got to Concord but did return to Lexington in time to witness the battle there.

The redcoats arrived in Lexington on the morning of April 19. About 70 patriots were ready, lined up on the village green, and the first battle of the Revolution began. No one knows who fired the first shot, but when the fighting stopped, eight patriots lay dead, and the redcoats had won.

The British marched on to Concord, sure that the militia there could be defeated as easily as the one at Lexington. But Prescott had arrived with his warning, and more than 300 patriots lay in wait at North Bridge. In the fighting, three redcoats and two rebels were killed. With more patriots arriving, the British turned around and retreated to Boston.

As the British marched back to Boston, they were met by patriots who had been roused by Revere, Dawes, and Prescott and were on their way to join the battle in Concord. When these patriots saw the British marching away from Concord, they attacked. By the time they reached Boston, the British had lost 200 men, and the Revolutionary War had begun.

Dedicated to my father, Frank Thompson. JT

To create his artwork, Jef Thompson first drew one element of each illustration,
then transferred and cut it into scratch board (a board covered in a white clay coated with ink).
The separate pieces (a man here, a tree there) were then scanned into a computer
and composed in a black and white image of the final illustration.
This black and white image was then colored using the computer program Adobe Photoshop.
A final image may have as many as ten different elements and, with colors added, may be 80 layers or more in depth.

Text is set in Matrix Tall from Emigre, altered by the designer. Title text is hand-lettered by Anita Karl, Compass Productions.
Book design by Bea Jackson, Ivy Pages.

Thank you to Patrick Leehey of the Paul Revere House in Boston, Massachusetts,
for his help with the map and the historical note.

ISBN 0-439-22617-1

Published by Scholastic Inc., 555 Broadway, New York, NY 10012,
by arrangement with the National Geographic Society.

12 11 10 9 8 7 6 5 4 3 2 1   0 1 2 3 4 5/0

Printed in the U.S.A.   14

First Scholastic printing, October 2000